⁊ *Speaking of Sin*

COWLEY PUBLICATIONS is a ministry of the brothers of the Society of Saint John the Evangelist, a monastic order in the Episcopal Church. Our mission is to provide books and resources for those seeking spiritual and theological formation. COWLEY PUBLICATIONS is committed to developing a new generation of writers and teachers who will encourage people to think and pray in new ways about spirituality, reconciliation, and the future.

·- BARBARA BROWN TAYLOR

Speaking of Sin

The Lost Language of Salvation

COWLEY PUBLICATIONS

Lanham, Chicago, New York, Toronto, and Plymouth, UK

Published by Cowley Publications
An imprint of Rowman & Littlefield Publishers, Inc.
A wholly owned subsidary of The Rowman & Littlefield Publishing Group, Inc.
4501 Forbes Boulevard, Suite 200
Lanham, MD 20706

Estover Road
Plymouth PL6 7PY
United Kingdom

Distributed by National Book Network

Library of Congress Cataloging-in-Publication Data:

Taylor, Barbara Brown.
    Speaking of Sin: the lost language of salvation / Barbara Brown Taylor.
        p.   cm.
    Includes bibliographical references.
    ISBN-10: 1-56101-189-4   ISBN-13: 978-1-56101-189-6   (alk. paper)
    1. Sin.   2. Salvation.   3. Christianity—Terminology.   I. Title.
    BT715.T23   2001
    234—dc21   00-047391

Biblical quotations are from the *New Revised Standard Version of the Bible,* © 1989,
by the Division of Christian Education of the National Council of the Churches
of Christ in the United States of America.

Cover design: Brad Norr Design
Interior design: Wendy Holdman

Printed in the United States of America.

∞™ The paper used in this publication meets the minimum requirements of
American National Standard for Information Sciences—Permanence of Paper
for Printed Library Materials, ANSI/NISO Z39.48-1992.

*For Harry Butman with
Respect and Affection*

Contents

Acknowledgments

The seed of this book was planted in the fall of 1999, when Erica Wood, Warden of the College of Preachers in Washington, D.C., invited me to deliver the annual Hastings Lecture at the National Cathedral. My topic was preaching repentance in an age of self-defense. I thank both Erica and her colleague Shelagh Casey Brown for that opportunity, as well as for long years of happy association with the College.

The following spring I was able to turn that one lecture into three when Coleman Markham invited me to give the Sprinkle Lectures at Barton College in Wilson, North Carolina, where he chairs the department of religion and philosophy. I am grateful to him both for his hospitality and for his fortitude in publicizing lecture titles that might have scared the faint-hearted away.

I also want to thank Ruth Culley for introducing me to the concept of restorative justice, and Diana Chambers for inviting me to worship with one of the congregations of the Church of the Savior in Washington, D.C. I am grateful to Ray Cleere, president of Piedmont College, for giving me a job that includes time to write, and to my students for keeping my feet on the ground. I am especially grateful to Judy Barber, Vijaya Kandala, Paul Duke, Tucker Stone, Habib Badr, and Earl Brown for their contributions to this effort.

As always, these acknowledgments conclude with thanks to my husband Ed, who has forgiven me seventy-times-seven through the years and has thereby taught me most of what I know about newness of life.

Barbara Brown Taylor
Clarkesville, Georgia
August 2000

Introduction

Speaking of Sin

⌐

THE LANGUAGE OF FAITH, LIKE ANY OTHER LAN-
guage, resounds with the lives of those who speak it. Visit
a Pentecostal church in rural Tennessee and you will hear a different vocabulary than you hear at the Episcopal Cathedral in
New York City. Even if some of the words are the same, they
may be used in different ways, depending on everything from
the local theological climate to the larger secular culture in which
a church exists. A word as basic as "baptism" can conjure half a
dozen disparate images. One hearer sees an infant in a long white
gown being sprinkled over a stone baptismal font, while another
imagines an adult standing waist deep in a river current. A third
might not think "water" at all, but "Holy Spirit," envisioning a
baptism that involves divine ecstasy and speaking in tongues.

There is also an evolution of religious language over time,
leaving some old words to become fossils as new ones spring up
to name new realities. Very few Christians today share Paul's passion for the religious issue of circumcision, although he addressed
it in at least seven of his letters. Likewise, Paul never spoke of
the doctrine of the Trinity, which did not enter the Christian
vocabulary until hundreds of years after his death. The definition
of "catholic" has undergone quite a few changes over the centu-
ries, as has the relatively new word "protestant." After Auschwitz,

"Holocaust" acquired a capital letter as the epitome of evil, caus-
ing many to question the whole notion of "divine providence."

Twentieth-century additions to the language of faith include
the lexicons of process, liberation, feminist, and womanist the-
ologies, as well as the new hybrid languages developing at the
crossroads of Christianity and science, psychology, and the other
world religions. Christian response to this explosion of language
is predictably mixed. Some leaders encourage believers to return
to their roots, reclaiming the ancient language of faith and teaching it to their children. Others note that the old words simply
do not work anymore—especially among the young—and that
fresh revelations from God deserve fresh language. Even words
as central to Christian tradition as "atonement" and "salvation"
are currently under revision, with intriguing new interpretations
being brought to light.

As a lover of language, it is hard for me to let go of many
words. My tongue longs for words that disappeared before I was
born. Forsooth! Benison. Vouchsafe. Perdition. Twenty years ago
now, I spent a summer in the Adirondacks with some Quaker
girls who said "thee" instead of "hey you."

"Would thee like to go swimming at the pond today?" one of
them asked me. It was such a soft and unexpected pronoun that
I had to stop for a moment and rethink who I was. No one had
ever called me "thee" before, but it made me feel so gentle and holy
that I thought I could get used to it. At the same time, I have a
terrible time trying to read Elizabethan English out loud. All of
those "eth" verb endings sound as strange to my ear as Castilian
Spanish must sound to someone from Mexico City. As lovely as
the language is, it is not my language. I do not think in it, dream
in it, or speak it with my neighbors. If it is going to be a living
language for me, then some translation must occur.

In this little book, I want to focus on a small cluster of words that seem to be hard for many people to pronounce, especially in twenty-first century North America. "Sin" heads the list, followed by "damnation," "repentance," "penance" and "salvation." The group also includes words that survive only in scripture, such as "iniquity" and "transgression." When these words are pronounced out loud, many of them sound like language from an earlier age, when human relationship with God was laced with blame and threat. As old as the words are, they are still redolent with guilt. We may not know exactly what they mean, but we know that they judge us. The most obvious solution to the discomfort they provoke is to stop saying them altogether, which is what many of us have done.

Fewer and fewer of us use the words in our prayers or conversations. Some of our churches have stopped using them as well, dropping the confession of sin from Sunday services in order to make worship a more positive experience. When we speak of God, we go straight for the grace. The story of the prodigal son is one of our favorite stories because it assures us that no matter how far we have gone from God and no matter what we have done, we are always welcome home. Jesus died with his arms wide open as an everlasting reminder of our pardon, and all who have been baptized in his name have received the forgiveness of sin. Why, then, should we speak of sin anymore? Why dwell on the failures God has promised to absolve?

The only reason I can think of is because we believe that God means to redeem the world through us. We have been chosen, in the language of Genesis, not only to be blessed but also to be a blessing to all the families of the earth. Our participation in that high calling requires us to understand God's grace as something more than the infinite remission of our sins. If we want to take part in the divine work of redemption, then we will also understand God's grace as the gift of regeneration—the very real possibility of new life right here on earth—complete with new vision, new values, and new behavior.

As wary as I am of pious calls to perfection, it does seem to me that too many of us have given up hope of new life for ourselves or for the families of the earth. It is easier (and less painful) for us to rely on God's forgiveness of our sins than it is to believe that God might support us to quit them. But how can we quit them if we have forgotten what they are called?

Abandoning the language of sin will not make sin go away. Human beings will continue to experience alienation, deformation, damnation, and death no matter what we call them. Abandoning the language will simply leave us speechless before them, and increase our denial of their presence in our lives. Ironically, it will also weaken the language of grace, since the full impact of forgiveness cannot be felt apart from the full impact of what has been forgiven.

Before he was welcomed home, the prodigal son "came to." He recognized his sin against his father. He prepared his confession. He left one way of life for another, ready to do penance when he arrived home. His father's kiss erased it all, but not because the son was innocent. The son was guilty and he knew it, which was what gave the kiss its power. Jesus' own kiss comes to us in the form of a cross. If we remain unaware of our collusion with the forces of death that put him there, then it will be very difficult for us to receive his absolution, with its stunning offer of new life.

This book is a work in progress, intended to raise more questions than it answers. My plan is first of all to talk about the lost language of sin and salvation. What are some of the trends that have led to the abandonment of those words, and what kinds of substitutes have we been offered? Next, I want to explore the kinds of real live human experiences that underlie the word "sin" and explain why I believe it is such a helpful, hopeful word.

Finally, I will end with a reflection on repentance, which is one human response to sin, and the one that the church exists to realize.

Throughout these pages, I hope that I never sound like someone who thinks she knows the mind of God. I am a pastoral theologian and not a systematic one. My concern lies with those who have felt the undertow of sin in their own lives but who may lack the language to speak of it, as well as with those for whom the language of sin has lost its soul. I am not ready to let go of these words. The realities they point to are still very much with us, and we need to know their names. Of all the ways I have been taught to speak of them, the church's way still seems the most hopeful to me. It is a way that leads through guilt to grace, with a reliable promise of new life to all those with the God-given courage to speak of sin.

One

The Lost Language of Salvation

I HAVE AT LEAST TWO RELATED CONCERNS ABOUT THE language of sin and salvation. The first is about how difficult it is to speak in mainline churches today. The second is about what we may lose if we forget how to speak it, because a language is not just a collection of words, easily replaceable by any other language. A language is a particular community's way of making meaning over time. It is shaped by that community's experience of reality. It is loaded with that community's values.

Last summer I sat on the stoop of a souvenir shop in Greece with the owner, who bemoaned the decline of the Greek language on the world scene. "My language is so beautiful," he said, "but so untranslatable. We have five different words for 'poetry,' but when Greek is translated into English they all end up as the same word. That is why there are so few famous Greek writers and poets today." When the language is translated, not only its beauty but also much of its reality is lost. For example, he said, what the world calls the Olympic "games" are no such thing.

"These events are not play," the shopkeeper said. "They are not sport."

"What are they, then?" I asked him.

"I cannot tell you in English," he said. "The Greek word for what happens at the Olympics has no English equivalent."

In the same way, I believe, there are words in the Christian language that have no equivalent in the other languages we speak, such as the languages of business, law, or psychology. When we lose the religious words, we lose the hold they have on the realities they represent. Sin does not translate simply as rule-breaking, for instance, any more than it translates as evidence of psychosis. It is a bigger word than that, with deeper roots, and if we drop it from our vocabulary then our language, not to mention our experience, will be diminished.

As I go along, you will notice that I seem to be speaking about individual sin one moment and corporate sin the next, and that I am not always careful to distinguish existential sin from particular sins of commission or omission. Part of that is because my mind works in spirals instead of straight lines, but part of it is the richness of the word itself. Like the word "poetry" in Greek, sin has many meanings for Christians. It is a word we use to name a wide variety of things, ranging from individual wrongdoing to social injustice to the built-in fallibility of being human. What is called sinful in one household of faith may not be called sinful in another. To be labeled a sinner may strike fear in one person's heart while it causes another to shrug her shoulders. That is why it is important to dig around the word in order to discover what is clinging to its roots.

Although I do not remember it, my first experience with sin happened when I was five weeks old. The year was 1951. The occasion was my baptism in the Roman Catholic Church, which was still on the far side of Vatican II. Since my mother was not Catholic, the sacrament took place in a side chapel. I was her first-born, and she was wildly in love with me. The way she tells the story, the priest took me from her arms and began saying all kinds of terrible things about me. He said that I was sinful through and through, that I had the devil in me, but—not to worry—the waters of baptism would soon wash me clean as snow.

"You were the best thing I had ever done," she says, still chilled by the memory. "The moment I got you back in my arms, I looked at your father and said, 'We're getting out of here and we're not ever coming back.'" True to her word, she did not present either of my two younger sisters for baptism when they were born and we stayed away from church for seven years. When we finally went back, we chose a Methodist church, where I do not remember ever hearing a word about sin.

While we did not use the word at home, I learned that there were things I could do to bring me closer to my parents (tell the truth, help around the house, keep an eye on my sisters) as well as things I could do to push them away (trash my room, break things, smoke cigarettes). I also learned that while a sincere apology might get their attention, it was changed behavior my parents wanted from me. To that end, they set up consequences for my actions, so that I could experience the results of my choices. When I was old enough, they invited me to start setting limits for myself, thus trusting me more than I trusted myself. They went to all of this trouble, they said, because they wanted me to grow up a human being and not a lout. When I began to read the Bible years later, I recognized the same pattern in God's relationship with Israel. Even without knowing the words, I had already learned a great deal about sin, judgment, confession, repentance, penance, grace, and salvation.

Other children I knew were not so lucky. They lived with people who believed you could beat the sin out of a child, and they spent most of their time in hell. If those spiritually battered souls had any appetite for God left when they grew up, then they had an enormous amount of work to do before they could conceive of anything close to a loving judge.

I received my first dose of corporate sin during the civil rights era, right after my family moved from Ohio to Alabama in 1962.

Since I was only eleven years old I did not know what to call it yet, but I could feel the visceral wave of rage and fear that moved through my sixth-grade classroom when Martin Luther King, Jr.'s name was mentioned. It was as if my classmates had reached some agreement about him while I was out of the room. I would have asked them what they were so mad about, only I was afraid that would just make them madder.

I heard the venom in the word "nigger" and I saw the hate on George Wallace's face when I watched the evening news. A year later, I was sitting by the window in Miss Wyatt's seventh-grade classroom when the principal's voice came over the intercom. He regretted to tell us, he said, that President Kennedy had been shot. I did not hear the rest of what he said because so many of my classmates were clapping and cheering. Even then, I knew that they were not individually mean people. They were caught up in something bigger than themselves, which they could not even see.

When I was sixteen, I visited a Baptist church with some of my friends and heard sin defined clearly for the first time. Sin was rebellion against God, which could take any number of forms. The youth minister warned us against drinking, drugs, and sex outside of marriage. He made sure we knew the Ten Commandments. He initiated us into a narrative worldview that went something like this:

No matter how hard we try, human beings are inherently corrupt. God made us and gave us paradise to live in, but the first woman led the first man to sin by feeding him the fruit of a forbidden tree. The first couple passed their rebelliousness on to their children, and ever since then sinning has come as naturally to us as breathing. There is no help for us within ourselves, and without help our souls are in mortal danger of hell. God tried all kinds of things to save us—commandments, prophets, plagues of locusts—but when none of those worked God finally sent his son to die on the cross for our sins. Those who believe in him are free from sin. God will not punish them for their wrongdoing, since Jesus consented to be punished in their place. Meanwhile, sin continues to cause Jesus great pain, which is why we must do our best to live sinless lives. If we continue to sin, then God will send us to hell for eternity. If we resist sin, then we will spend eternity in heaven with Jesus.

This story was communicated to me with such genuine passion for my salvation that I joined the church and was baptized again by immersion. The church became my safe haven where I spent all day every Sunday and most Wednesday nights. It felt so safe to me that one Sunday night I brought a couple of runaway boys with long hair to church in hopes of finding them a place to stay. Before the evening was over, we were all turned out into the night and asked not to come back. It was a stunning reversal for me. With no warning I could discern, I became one of the sinners the preacher had been warning me about, and I experienced the full absence of grace.

I stayed away from church for two years after that, until I entered college and discovered university worship. The liturgy was different every week. The music was contemporary and the sermons were short. What was not to like? With the chaplain's sanction, students gathered to discuss things that would have made the walls of my old Baptist church fall down. As long as two people were single and careful, what was wrong with sex outside of marriage? Was it really wrong to dodge the draft, or was it even more wrong to put on a uniform and kill people for pay? What was more wrong, to have an abortion, or to bring an unwanted baby into an already overpopulated world?

None of these discussions took place under the rubric of sin. The operative phrase on campus was "moral and ethical decision-making." There is nothing wrong with that phrase, as far as I am concerned. It suggests standards for human behavior without making assumptions about religious faith. Learning to use the phrase, I understood that there were immoral and unethical decisions I could make that would violate basic human values. When I substituted the word "sin," however, the stakes automatically went up. If I sinned, then the values in question were no longer human values but God's values. Sinning sounded a lot more serious to me than making a poor moral decision.

In seminary I learned to think more academically about sin. I read Paul, Luther, Tillich, and Barth. I learned to hear the difference between *sin* and *sins*—*sin* being the existential state of distance from God and *sins* being the willful human choices that maintain that distance. I also joined the Episcopal Church, where I learned the confession from the 1928 prayer book by heart:

> Almighty God, Father of our Lord Jesus Christ, maker of all things, judge of all men: We acknowledge and bewail our manifold sins and wickedness, which we from time to time most grievously have committed, by thought, word, and deed, against thy divine Majesty, provoking most justly thy wrath and indignation against us.[1]

While the aesthetics were vastly different from the Baptist church of my teenage years, the message was roughly the same. I was a miserable sinner, who was not worthy to gather up the crumbs under God's table. While such a stark confession upset the positive self-image I was working so hard to generate in those days, it was also oddly comforting. Saying those words, I knew that there was nowhere lower to go. It was like sinking through sewage-filled water until I hit bottom, where I found the solid footing I needed to fight my way back toward the light.

I also knew that I was confessing more sin than I knew about, and more sins than my own. The language of the confession was plural, not singular. I happened to be among those who were in church saying it, but I knew that we said it on behalf of our whole species. However innocent any one of us may have believed ourselves to be, our collective rap sheet was pretty long. As a species, we needed all the forgiveness God was willing to give. Before long, I discovered more than I wanted to know about my own participation in collective sin.

Most theological education has a component called "supervised ministry." How that is defined and done differs from place to place, but in general it is hard to get through it without a broader understanding of the human condition. My own experience with it came after seminary, in a program designed to help people like me decide whether or not we had a vocation in ordained ministry. The first term was a breeze. My classmates and I were sent to hospitals, nursing homes, and rehabilitation centers, where we were given chaplains' badges and learned how to go from room to room delivering pastoral care. While we were so green that we made plenty of people feel worse instead of better, we had a pretty good handle on what we were supposed to do. We were supposed to establish rapport with people, one-on-one. We were supposed to enter into relationships with them that might help God heal them, by ministering to them in Jesus' name. The focus that term was on reflective listening and bedside manner.

The second term was a whole different thing. Our placements included soup kitchens, night shelters, and urban training centers, where we were encouraged to look past the individuals we served to the systems in which they were trapped. Slowly, reluctantly, we began to see that the little bit of good we could do one-on-one was regularly being swallowed up by the larger realities of people's lives. That was when I learned about how banks redlined neighborhoods, refusing to lend money to anyone whose

skin color or ethnic origin might lower property values. That was
when I learned that if you do not have a car or a permanent ad-
dress, then you are not going to get a job outside of a labor pool,
which will make sure you earn so little money that you have to
keep coming back. That was when I learned that a single mother
with six kids could lose her whole welfare check if her sixteen-
year old daughter got a part time job at the Burger King.

It was a hard term, because none of us knew how to tackle
those huge realities, but at the same time we could no longer ignore them. Those powers did more real harm to people's spirits
than we could begin to repair in our six or eight hours a week.
They sucked the hope right out of people. They taught people
not to trust. Worst of all, they treated human beings like human
trash, until the human beings began to believe them. Most days,
all we did was bandage them up and send them back out on the
streets, so that they could get chewed up all over again.

The third term, we were assigned to churches throughout the
community, where we essentially returned to the skills we learned
in term one. A few congregations had food pantries and clothes
closets—bandage ministries—but none of them knew any better
than we did how to tackle the larger systemic problems that made
those ministries necessary. Plus, while no one disagreed about
the goodness of handing out free food and clothes, quite a lot of
people disagreed about the rightness of petitioning the county
commission for more federal housing money or talking with local
utility companies about lowering their deposits for low income
families. Handing out free food and clothes was a charitable act.
Approaching the powers was a political act. We could give people
fish, but we could not ask why they had no fish.

After I was ordained, I was blessed with ten years in an urban
church that did both. During that time I was tempted almost
daily by sins of omission. I envied people whose jobs did not

include learning the names of the men who slept in the bushes outside their windows. I coveted an office on the top floor of some tall building, where I could become resigned to what was happening on the distant streets below. I understood why people moved to the suburbs and then voted against linking up with the rapid transit system that might bring scary people to their neighborhoods. Fortunately, my office remained on the ground floor of a downtown church that expected me to seek and serve Christ in all persons, loving my neighbor as myself. I remained aware enough of social sins to be surprised when religious people wanted to focus on sexual sins instead. I suppose that when poverty, crime, and degradation of the environment start looking unbeatable, then it is predictable that people will shift their attention to an enemy who seems easier to attack.

Eight years ago I moved to the country, where the language of sin is still widely spoken. It is heard mostly in the small, independent churches that dot the countryside, however, and not in the mainline churches. The language in mainline churches is about church growth, outreach, and denominational initiatives. Many of those churches are losing members, and they cannot afford language that might put people off. People do not want to hear about sin and repentance, after all. People want to hear about grace and forgiveness, although it is hard to imagine what those words might mean apart from the somber reality of sin.

That is enough of my own history of sin. I offer it in hopes that you will think about your own. I also confess it so that you will know why I am a little jumpy about the language of sin and salvation. Even when I hear it now from some of my students, I am aware of what an exclusive and sometimes abusive language it is. In the first place, it really only works with the initiated—that is, with people who have already bought into a worldview that includes a heaven, a hell, and a God who sends people one place or another. For people who have never been initiated into that worldview—or who have lived there and left—the language has little power, except perhaps as a deterrent to faith. People hear the guilt coming and they leave the room. They are tired of being judged and threatened by Christians who say "love" and do fear.

In the second place, the language always comes embedded with a set of cultural values. Sin often turns out to be whatever a particular group disapproves of, with wide variation due to class, creed, and ethnicity. Selective Bible passages may be offered to support a group's definitions, but there is little awareness that God's values may turn out to be different from their own.

According to the most recent Gallup poll, 95 percent of United States residents continue to believe in God. They simply stop going to church, where the language they hear about God neither matches the reality of their lives nor feeds the hunger of their hearts. They design their own worldviews, consciously or unconsciously, piecing together things that make sense to them from various sacred and secular traditions. Along the way, they acquire new language that better describes the world as they understand it, and many of them never darken the doorway of a church again.

One of my students, a Congregational minister's son, finds the Tibetan Buddhist dharma of compassion much more compelling than the Christian law of love. Another has become a proud and very verbal Wiccan, while a third says that he has discovered more community in his weekly AA meeting than he ever felt in church. To use my own language, what I believe each of these young people is seeking is some kind of salvation—that is, a transformed way of life in the world that is characterized by peace, meaning, and freedom. In the search process, each has come up against the interior and exterior obstacles to that way of life—what I would call sin—and each has discovered some new tools for surmounting those obstacles. While only the AA student might recognize the word "repentance" (which I am pretty sure he would rather call "Step Six"), they are all involved in turning away from an old way of life and turning toward a new way that promises them more abundant life.

My curiosity as a Christian—and also, to be honest, my sorrow—is about how the language of the church failed them so badly that they have decided to look elsewhere for life. How did those of us who speak the language of faith manage to turn words such as "sin" and "salvation" into clichés? How did we manage to empty them of their power? I am not sure I can answer that question, but I think I can at least identify some of the trends that have led to the lost language of salvation.

The three trends I want to talk about are pluralism, postmodernism, and secularism. I am not sure they can really be separated, since each has implications for the other, but they are all descriptive of the religious landscape at the beginning of the twenty-first century. I do not think of any of them as bad things, necessarily. They may even be good things, insofar as they push us to clarify and refresh the language of faith. All I know for sure is that we cannot afford to ignore them. If we want our language to survive, then we are going to have to recognize and respond to their challenges by entering into dialog with them.

I think of pluralism as spiritual globalization. With the media presently available to us, we know more about other world religions than we have ever known before. His Holiness the Dalai Lama has written books on the *New York Times* bestseller list. You may join an electronic ashram on the World Wide Web, or request materials from the International Society for Krishna Consciousness. You may take a class in Hatha Yoga or Tai Chi at your local YMCA, or join a transcendental meditation group sponsored by the followers of the Maharishi Mahesh Yogi. You may also remain ignorant of such things if you like, but if you do, then you will not have anything very intelligent to say when someone asks you to help her think through the differences between the Buddha's Four Noble Truths and Jesus' Sermon on the Mount, or wants to know why Islam and Judaism agree that Christianity is not a monotheistic religion.

I am not suggesting that anyone learn more about world religions in order to subvert them. Sacred truth is a very deep well into which human beings have been lowering leaky buckets for millennia. The more we learn about what other traditions have fetched up, the more we learn about our own. It is helpful, for instance, since Jesus was a Jew, to know that Judaism has no doctrine of original sin, and that salvation is conceived of as life lived in obedience to Torah. Heaven and hell have never been very lively concepts for most Jews, who find the Christian focus on the world to come more than a little irrelevant. The point of human life on earth, as any son or daughter of Torah can tell you, is to assist God in the redeeming of this world now.

It is also helpful to know that most eastern religions have very little to say about God at all. The Buddha taught that theological speculation is about as useful as wondering what kind of arrow has struck you in the chest. You may measure it if you want to. You may develop theories about where it came from, who shot it, and what kind of wood it is made from, but all in all your time would be better spent deciding how you are going to remove it from your body. The focus is not on orthodoxy—right belief—but on orthopraxis—right practice—which strikes me as a refreshing alternative to the heresy trials that have plagued my own denomination in recent years. Sin, in Buddhist teaching, is ignorance about the true nature of reality, and salvation is a matter of removing the arrow, or waking up.

I cannot imagine getting away with many references to other

world religions from the pulpit. (I once said "Sufi" in a sermon at a Presbyterian seminary and watched a whole room full of eyes narrow at the same time.) But I do believe that learning other languages has helped me to speak my own more fluently. It has also helped me speak more respectfully with people of other faiths. Even in tiny Clarkesville, Georgia, I live and work with Muslims, Hindus, Buddhists, and Jews. Their presence reminds me that religion is not singular, but plural—and that if I want my Christian language to remain lively, then I had better learn some words from their languages as well.

So spiritual globalization is one trend that has affected the language of sin and salvation. People are discovering other languages that make equal or more sense to them, and unless we know a little something about those languages too, we will not be able to enter into dialog with them.

A second major trend is postmodernism, which has been used by so many people to describe so many different things that we may be excused for wondering if anyone can really define it at all. My own working definition of it is that the modern age is over—the age in which we believed in the power of the state, or the academy, or the church to bring out the best in us. In the age just past, nationalism has brought us Hitler, science has brought us the atom bomb, and religion has brought us some really awful television programming, not to mention apartheid or the civil war in Northern Ireland. Humanity has turned out to be hard to perfect, and the old structures we relied on to do so have let us down.

The postmodern age is an age of disillusionment with once revered authorities, which is not an entirely bad thing. Does anyone want to live life under illusion? No, not really. It is best for illusions to be revealed for what they are. Meanwhile, disillusioned people respond in all sorts of ways. Some abandon the search for meaning altogether, while others hunt for deeper and more reliable sources of it. Some campaign for a return to the values of the past, while others invest themselves in new visions of the future.

One characteristic of postmodernism is distrust of the old institutions that have let people down. In my home county, only about a third of the registered voters show up to cast ballots in any given election. Home schooling has become a nationwide phenomenon, and I do not expect membership in mainline churches to zoom up any time soon. The authority of the pulpit has been eroded, along with the authority of the presidency and the public school system, as well as almost every other institution I can think of at the moment.

What this means for the language of sin and salvation, I believe, is that many people are no longer willing to take the church's word on those things. The threat of sin and the promise of salvation sound too much like part of the old control mechanism for keeping people in line, which has failed even at the highest echelons of church leadership. For the culture at large, religious language has been replaced by the language of spirituality, which uses gentler words such as "stress-reduction," "empowerment," and "harmony." While I have nothing against such words, I am not sure that they are adequate to describe the darker realms of human experience, where power is a problem, not an asset, and where harmony is a distant memory from a life that ended a long time ago.

In a postmodern age, the language of sin and salvation will only communicate with the disillusioned if it is absolutely truthful about the realities of their lives, and if it supports them to name those realities for themselves. The days are long gone when most preachers can stand up in pulpits and name people's sins for them. They do not have that authority anymore. What they can do, I believe, is to describe the experience of sin and its aftermath so vividly that people can identify its presence in their own lives, not as a chronic source of guilt, nor as sure proof that they are inherently bad, but as the part of their individual and corporate lives that is crying out for change.

A third trend, which is woven through the other two, is secularism. This comes in so many forms that you might as well call it present day life on earth, which is why it has had such terrific impact on the language of sin and salvation.

In a recent issue of *Harper's Magazine*, Lewis Lapham proposes a merger of the seven cardinal virtues with the seven deadly sins. His argument is that heaven and heaven's values have become redundant to North Americans who have created their own heavens on earth. Virtues do not meet the requirements of the global market, he explains, while sins sustain the stock market, keep employment rates high, excite speculation, and satisfy the public appetite for sexual and political intrigue. "Trim out the fat of the seven virtues," he says, "and nothing bad happens to the price of real estate or the Dow Jones Industrial Average; take away the seven deadly sins, and the country goes promptly broke."[2]

His satirical solution is to downsize the virtues by recognizing the practical virtues of sin. Pride moves people to endow named scholarship funds, he points out, while anger and lust fuel the entertainment industry. But I believe that the culture has already devised its own solution by downsizing the number of things we call sin. Suicide, divorce, and addiction are no longer considered sinful by large segments of the population. Nor are cohabitation and having children out of wedlock. Sex before marriage is so routine that virgin brides and grooms are as rare as comets. We call lying "spin" and greed "motivation." What is to be gained from condemning such things, when people are going to do them anyway? Why not respect the individual's freedom to choose, since it is the individual who will bear the consequences?

I like to call this the "de-evolution" of sin, which is as apparent in church circles as it is in the culture at large. Sabbath-breaking and image-making were once punishable by death. Nowadays few church people think twice about mowing the lawn on Sunday or printing a picture of the crucified Christ on a polyester tee shirt. Usury and gluttony have ceased to be serious sins, along with swearing and gambling. What mainline church could afford to ban bankers, big eaters, or lottery players from leadership roles? Add to this the different codes of conduct encountered by Christians who may change denominations—moving from a tradition in which drinking alcohol is considered sinful, for instance, to one in which alcohol is used in worship—and the slope becomes exceedingly slippery. In many congregations, the only sins openly denounced from the pulpit are low attendance, poor stewardship, and failure to sign up for the Sunday school rota.

One of the more interesting effects of secularism on the language of sin and salvation has been the replacement of that language with the languages of medicine and law. Karl Menninger was among the first to document this change in a 1973 bestseller called *Whatever Became of Sin?* As a psychiatrist, Menninger freely admitted that existential sin was not his area. He was more interested in wrongdoing, which he defined broadly as "failure to realize in conduct and character the moral ideal, at least as fully as possible under existing circumstances."[3] His interest grew as much from his work with prisoners as it did from his work with psychiatric patients. In both cases, he wanted to understand as much as he could about why some people engage in destructive behavior as well as how other people try to control that behavior.

Recalling the harshness with which sin was once punished—locking sinners in stocks in the town square, for instance, or branding their cheeks with monograms of their sins—Menninger suggested that at least one reason for the de-evolution of sin has been loss of public support for such cruel and unusual punishment. Another has been growing public awareness that "sin" can turn out to be whatever the dominant religious culture disapproves of, making it one more tool of oppression. In the pre-Civil War south, a slave's rebellion against a master was regarded as sin. In the rural south where I live, a woman's call to preach is still regarded by many as sin. In light of such judgments, large numbers of people have simply stopped calling some things sin. The really awful things are turned over to the courts as crimes, while the more self-destructive things are turned over to the medical establishment as mental illnesses, leaving a great deal in the middle to become strictly personal matters.

Meanwhile, Menninger said, the disappearance of the word "sin" involves a shift in the allocation of responsibility for evil. By most definitions, wrongdoing (a.k.a. sin) involves choice. You know that stealing the candy bar is wrong but you do it anyway, and when your mother finds out about it, she is going to make you go back to the store, tell the manager what you have done, and pay for the candy bar. This is a type of repentance: to turn around, to confess, to make amends, and—presumably—to be restored to fullness of life. Your mother may have made you do it, but by teaching you the pattern she hoped that you would one day do it for yourself, when it would not depend on her but on your own sense of having done wrong.

If you continued to steal candy bars, however, the situation would become more problematic. Your mother might decide to nip your criminal tendencies in the bud by asking a friendly policeman to stop by the house and make a mock arrest. Or she might notice that the thefts occurred on the same weekends that your father called to say he would not be coming home, leading her to send you to a counselor instead. She might even blame herself for not making you go to Sunday school, and volunteer to go with you to see a local pastor.

In general, Menninger says, the distinction between crime, sickness, and sin is the professional management the subject receives—that is, what kind of rescuer is chosen to do something about the failure to realize the moral ideal. Choose the policeman and the paradigm for the failure is crime and punishment. Choose the counselor and the model becomes sickness and cure. Choose the pastor and you choose the language of sin and repentance. Of the three, the medical model is the least punitive.

What sense would it make to punish someone who is mentally ill, or to ask someone to repent of a symptom? Unlike crime or sin, illness does not carry the onus of choice. The responsibility for evil, or wrongdoing, is shifted elsewhere—to biochemistry, to abusive parents, to birth defects and head injuries. In our legal system, wrongdoers who can demonstrate illness receive treatment instead of punishment. Even those who are not ill may hope for less severe punishment if they can demonstrate that they were not entirely responsible for their actions.

"Your honor, I was following the orders of my military superior."

"I didn't mean to kill him. We were just a bunch of guys out having a good time. Then he made a pass at me and it was like my head exploded."

"Yes ma'am, I see the picture, and I know that's me, but I don't even remember being there that night. I had just come off a double shift at the plant, I was on pain pills for my back, and I should never have started drinking on top of all those pills."

The truth in statements such as these is that none of us acts in a vacuum. Our lives are fundamentally linked with all other lives. Our choices are limited by other people's choices, as well as by many factors beyond our control, including gender, class, race, and culture. Meanwhile, some things seem to happen without conscious choice on our parts. We "find ourselves" striking out, breaking things, shaking babies who will not stop crying. The consequences of our actions are the same whether we meant to or not, but to admit that we are responsible may not match how we felt at the time.

"Responsible" sounds so conscious, so free and powerful. On the contrary, many of us upon reflection would say that when we engaged in wrongdoing we felt bewildered, scared, and weak. We did the awful things we did because at the moment they offered us our best shot at survival. In a pinch, hurting is preferable to being hurt, having to not having, and staying alive by any means is preferable to dying. Because such decisions seem driven more by necessity than by choice, we may opt for the language of self-defense. I did not mean to. I had to. Anyone in my position would have done the same thing.

Sometimes the self-defense can take on a strident tone. Instead of protesting that they had no choice, the accused may insist that they made the right (or at least the best) choice.

"I did what I had to do under the circumstances."

"He should never have touched me like that."

"Anyone with that much money deserves to be robbed."

Either way, the point is to shift responsibility for failure elsewhere—to enter a "not guilty" plea in hopes of avoiding punishment altogether or at least receiving a reduced sentence. In Milwaukee last November, a federal judge set aside the murder conviction of a woman who had killed a teenage girl in 1991. What was her defense? Post-traumatic stress incurred from overexposure to urban violence.

Maybe those of us in the church have watched too many courtroom dramas on television. Maybe we have spent too much

money on self-help books, or maybe we have just forgotten how
to speak our own language. However it has happened, we seem
to have abandoned our own paradigm for dealing with human
failure in favor of the medical and legal paradigms.

I can think of at least two phenomena over the past fifty years
that have aided the erosion of theological language in this regard.
With the addition of clinical pastoral education to seminary cur-
ricula, theology students were introduced to the language of depth
psychology. Books by Freud and Erickson appeared on shelves
once ruled by Tillich and Barth. Diagnostic manuals provided far
more detail than most pastoral care texts. To sit down to talk with
a troubled person was one thing, but to be able to recognize signs
of manic-depression or narcissistic personality disorder in that
person—well! That was to feel like a true professional. Clergy
seized on the language of sickness and health, not only because
it offered them a fresh perspective on their work, but also because
it promised better results than the language they had been using.

More recently, clergy have had to learn the language of the law
as well. If a distraught parent comes to see me and begins to tell
me about her irrationally violent feelings toward her child, I stop
her and tell her that our conversation is no longer confidential. If
she says anything that leads me to believe her child is in danger,
then I am required by law to call the Department of Family and
Children Services. The same is true if someone threatens suicide
or murder in my hearing. If a life is in danger, then I have to
call the police—both to save the life and to avoid being sued for
professional malpractice myself. In order to secure malpractice
insurance for my parish, I have to know how to read the policy
manual, interpret it to my lay leaders, and get signed affidavits
from each of them that the church is in full compliance.

In many ways, I am grateful to have learned these other languages. Since they are dominant languages in my culture, it is

good for me to know them. What I am not yet ready to do is to abandon my own language, which offers a different paradigm for human failure and recovery.

As Paul Tillich wrote almost thirty years ago, the great words of our religious tradition cannot be replaced. There are no adequate substitutes for them, and when we try to talk around them, we find our speech diminished. Replacing sin with "pathology" and repentance with "recovery" may make us feel better, but it will be hard for us to find this vocabulary in scripture. We may also discover that we have exchanged a deeply nuanced language for a much shallower one, and that our experience flattens out to match the language we have chosen.

This connection between the language and the experience it describes is crucial, I think. One way to explain why the language of sin and salvation does not "work" anymore is that such congruence has been lost. The words have come unstitched from the life events they once described, leaving the words bereft of meaning for many hearers. "But there *is* a way of re-discovering their meaning," according to Tillich, "the same way that leads us down into the depth of our human existence. In that depth these words were conceived; and there they gained power for all ages; there they must be found again by each generation, and by each of us for himself."[4]

In order to speak of sin in any compelling way, we need to go diving for the core experiences that word names. If we do, then we may just discover that sin is our only hope.

Two

Sin Is Our Only Hope

⌐

ONCE UPON A TIME, AN ESKIMO HUNTER WENT TO see the local missionary who had been preaching in his village.

"I want to ask you something," the hunter said.

"What's that?" the missionary said.

"If I did not know about God and sin," the hunter said, "would I go to hell?"

"No," the missionary said, "not if you did not know."

"Then why," asked the hunter, "did you tell me?"

Annie Dillard tells the story in her book *Pilgrim at Tinker Creek*, where it serves as riddle about the mystery of sin and salvation. What the story suggests is that God, sin, and hell are things that do not exist unless a missionary comes to town and starts preaching about them.

Certainly, the preacher imports a theory about how those things relate to one another. If you know about A and B, then you are liable for C. If, on the other hand, you do not know about A and B, then you are excused from C. The possession of such divine equations is one way preachers have managed to stay in business all these years. We are also big on definitions. If you are not sure what A, B, and C really mean, then you had better come listen to us. We can tell you who God is, what sin is, and how both of those can land you in hell—information that is essential for the health of your eternal soul.

But while preachers may import the theories and define the terms of sin and salvation, we do not invent the realities that the words name. Long before there were preachers, churches, or even organized religions, there were essential human experiences of community and alienation, of connection and disconnection to the divine. You can find paintings of those experiences on the walls of prehistoric caves, and hear richly symbolic stories about them that pre-date written language. Different wisdom traditions give different names to those experiences and offer different understandings of them, but the experiences themselves are the realities that give rise to all the theories and definitions.

Before there was any such thing as a Christian doctrine of original sin, for instance, there was a story about a man and a woman—the first man and woman—who lived in a beautiful garden full of peacocks and calla lilies and panda bears. This paradise contained everything their hearts could desire, including the close, sheltering presence of God. There was only one thing in the whole garden that they could not have, only one thing that God had commanded them to leave alone, and that was God's own tree. "You may freely eat of every tree in the garden," God had told them, "but of the tree of the knowledge of good and evil you shall not eat, for in the day that you eat of it you shall die" (Genesis 2:16-17).

So of course from that moment on it was the only thing they wanted. The fruit of that tree probably tasted better than the fruit of all the other trees combined. It probably tasted like a cross between fresh pineapple and ripe cherries. Plus, it clearly had magical powers. Eating that fruit was what made God God, which was why God did not want them to go anywhere near it. Or at least that was what the snake said.

The snake was a marvelous creature, with a tongue like a pink silk banner that rippled as he spoke. He took a real interest in Adam and Eve. He explained things to them, whereas God had not. All God had really told them was to stay away from the tree, but the snake told them why. "You will not die," the snake said, "for God knows that when you eat of it your eyes will be opened, and you will be like God, knowing good and evil" (Genesis 3:4-5). Then the snake left Adam and Eve alone to make up their own minds.

It did not take them long. In the first recorded act of human initiative, they decided for themselves what was best for them. They exercised their freedom to disobey God's command, ate the fruit, and wound up standing on the curb outside the garden with their battered suitcases lying beside them on the ground.

The snake was right—they did not die as God had said, but it was the end of life as they had known it. In one afternoon they lost everything: their paradise, their innocence, their intimacy with God. All it took was one stupid, willful decision, and there was no going back. They had acquired the knowledge of good and evil, along with the knowledge of which one they had chosen. From the moment they left the garden, life was hard. Life was painful. Life was forever out of whack.

If we continue to tell the story, that is because it continues to be true for us. Almost everyone can remember his or her own loss of innocence: the first time you saw your father's change lying on his bureau and slid a quarter into your own pocket, only to turn around and find him standing by the door; or the first time your mother caught you in the basement playing doctor with your friends.

I remember watching a grandfather play in a swimming pool with his first boy grandchild, who was about two years old at the time. The boy was big for his age and a real handful, try-ing to writhe out of his grandfather's arms in order to test the waters for himself. His grandfather held on to him, afraid that he would drown, but the more he tried to hang on, the harder the child pushed away. Finally the boy scooped up a handful of water and flung it at his grandfather, only he misjudged the distance and wound up slapping him in the face. I remember the smack, then the silence, then the roar.

In a flash of anger, his grandfather shouted at him and shook him hard. The boy went limp and silent in his arms. He had never heard his grandfather's voice like that, had never been hurt by him in any way. Looking on, I saw their primal relationship ruptured in that moment. Their perfect bond was broken, and while the moment passed, things were never the same again. The child had lost his innocence. Between his past and his present life with his grandfather there was a sword flaming and turning to guard the way to the tree of life.

Some of these early Eden experiences include willful disobedience, but many of them do not. As C. S. Lewis once pointed out, our first knowledge of punishment often precedes our first knowledge of having done anything wrong. Like Adam and Eve, we are mere innocents exploring the territory. Even words as clear as "Don't eat that" do not mean anything until we have in fact eaten it, and thus discover the consequences of our actions for the first time. Did any one of you fully understand the command, "Don't touch the hot stove, sweetie" until you were nursing a red-hot blister on your hand?

The apparent inevitability of Adam and Eve's decision makes their story even more compelling. If God did not want them to eat from the tree, then why did God put it there in the first place? And who dreamed up that talking snake? If it was all a test of the first couple's obedience, then why didn't God let them work up to it a little? You know, start off with something less significant, such as "Don't call me after 9 P.M." or "Remember to feed the goldfish"?

Adam and Eve were still trying to remember the names of things when they were presented with their first moral choice. Their skin had barely dried off yet. They made the wrong choice, but there is hardly a human being alive who does not understand why. Innocence is so fragile, so curious, so *dumb*. Choosing God cannot be the same thing as staying innocent. If it is, then there is no hope for any of us.

Some lovers of this story say that Adam and Eve were destined to do what they did—not because of original sin but because of God. God knew that they had to eat the fruit. It was the only way for them to wake up, so that they could make real choices from then on.

It is a wonderful story, not because there are no problems in it but because it tells the truth about the way things really are. We really are free to make disastrous decisions. Our choices really do have consequences. And there really are some flaws in the whole setup, whether they come in the form of talking snakes or in the form of this almost biological urge we have to choose things that we know are ruinous for us and for the whole creation.

But nowhere in this story is the world "sin" mentioned, much less the phrase "original sin." That tag line was assigned to the story much later—in the fourth century C.E.—by Augustine of Hippo, who turned the tale of Adam and Eve into an explanation for the human tendency to choose evil instead of good. Largely through his influence, the Eden story has become the archetypal story of sin for Christianity, leading many of us to think of sin primarily as individual disobedience.

The Bible will not support such a simple understanding. There is also the great sin at Sinai, when an entire people chose to worship a golden calf they could see in lieu of a sovereign God they could not. There is the sin of the sons of Eli, who helped themselves to the best cuts of meat from offerings meant for God

(1 Samuel 2:17), and the sin of Saul's troops, who ate meat without first draining the blood from it (1 Samuel 14:33). There are sins so endemic to certain places that they are called the sins of Sodom and Gomorrah, or Ninevah, or Judah. There are certainly sexual sins, as in Amnon's rape of his half-sister Tamar (2 Samuel 13), or David's affair with Bathsheba (2 Samuel 11), but there are also sins of the rich against the poor (Amos 4:1), as well as the sins of those who have more faith in military might (Amos 3:11) or religion (Amos 5:21) than they do in God.

Individual disobedience is only one facet of sin in the Hebrew Bible, which uses three different words for the act of separation from God. The first word (and by far the most often used) comes from the root *chatah*, "to miss a mark." While it is used for sins as intentional as David's plot to kill Bathsheba's husband Uriah (2 Samuel 11:14-15), or Jeroboam's decision to set up golden calves in the northern cities of Bethel and Dan (1 Kings 12:29), it retains the sense of going astray. David and Jeroboam did not set out to do wrong. They both started out as leaders chosen by God to do right, but along the way they got distracted. Other things drew their attention away from God, and they missed the mark.

The second Hebrew word comes from the root *avah*, "to act wrongly." Translated most often as "iniquity," this separation from God includes wrong intent, and usually involves violation of the commandments. When Eli's sons steal meat from God, they commit iniquity. So do the people of Israel, when they prefer the sweet favors of Baal or Asherah to the stern justice of Yahweh.

The third word comes from the root *pasha*, "to rebel." Most often translated as "transgression," it is often paired with the second word, as in "iniquities and transgressions." This separation from God is full-fledged revolt. Among the transgressions denounced by Micah are foreclosures by wealthy landowners who turn poor people out of their homes, unjust laws that hit women and children hardest, and preachers who say whatever people want to hear.

What links all three of these Hebrew words together is their common theme of going against God's will. Whether people are missing a mark, acting wrongly, or engaging in outright rebellion, they are out of sync with God. They have wandered far in a land that is waste, and God's judgment is not so much some kind of extra punishment God dumps on them as it is God's announcement that they have abandoned the way of life. Like some divine *jiu-jitsu,* master, God does not set out to hurt them. God simply spins their rejection of life around so that they can feel the full force of it for themselves.

Once, when a friend and I were driving to another state, we began a long and rambling conversation about hell. Neither of us bought the picture we had grown up with of a fiery torture chamber presided over by God's own storm troopers. But we did share the sense of justice that underlies that picture, and we had both made enough bad choices in our lives to know about their consequences.

"The thing is," my friend said, "in this life, it's possible to get away with some of the awful stuff we do for a long time. We can hide it or lie about it and sometimes it takes years for the fallout to catch up with us. But in God's life, everything is present and revealed. When you make a choice, there is absolutely no delay in feeling the consequences of it. The moment you think or speak or act, you get a full dose of the reality you have just chosen." We put the car on cruise control and chased that idea around for a while.

"So if I choose hate," I said, "then my heart gets wrapped in barbed wire right that minute, and I can feel every one of those spikes gouging me?"

"Worse than that," she said. "All around you, crowds of angry people you can't see are screaming vile things at you. They are punching you and kicking you in the dark, because one of the main consequences of hating is finding out how it feels to be hated."

"That sounds like hell," I said, "but is it now or later?"

"I guess that it's whenever your consequences catch up with you," she said. "The more you're living God's life, though, the quicker they come and the worse they hurt."

"You make it sound like hell is a function of getting closer to God instead of further away."

"Well maybe it is. Maybe it's God's grace to let us feel hell so acutely that we decide we don't want to live there anymore."

"Then we can get out once we're in?"

"You're asking the wrong person. Do I look like God?"

When the Hebrew Bible was translated into Greek, *chatah* won out over the other Hebrew verbs, so that "missing the mark" became the main sense of sin that was carried into the New Testament. While sin is sometimes spoken of in the gospels as a debt (as you can hear in both Matthew and Luke's versions of the Lord's prayer), the emphasis is no longer on specific human misdeeds but on a state or power of darkness that separates human beings from God. While Judaism's solution to that darkness was following Torah, Jesus became the embodiment of Torah for Christianity, so that following him became the Christian way of safety—or salvation—from sin.

For some people, however, Jesus' victory over sin became a substitute for their own. When I was at Yale Divinity School in the 1970s, I remember becoming irate because the books I wanted were never in the library, nor was there any record at the front desk that they had been checked out. When I asked the librarian what was going on, he told me that the Divinity School had the highest theft rate of any graduate school in the university.

"How embarrassing," I said. "Why do you suppose that is?"

"Grace," he said, with a rueful look on his face. "You guys

figure all has been forgiven ahead of time, so you go ahead and take what you want."

I did not preach about it in chapel the next week. It would have sounded petty, for one thing, to preach about stolen library books while broken soldiers were still being shipped home from Vietnam. For another thing, I had not accumulated much evidence that preaching against sin really worked. When people tried it on me, I usually went somewhere else in my head, managing to look remorseful while I was actually weighing the merits of meatloaf versus spaghetti for supper.

It was the guilt that sent me packing. I already had a full load of guilt about everything from my weight to my prayer life. One more ounce of guilt and the pew would have collapsed underneath me, dumping me right on the floor. Plus, the things that the preacher wanted me to feel guilty about were not often high on my list of concerns. Even the worthy things, such as apartheid and the hole in the ozone layer, seemed so far away that I could hardly grasp them, while some of the other things, such as the evils of Halloween and bingo, just struck me as inane. It was easy to see that the preacher was worked up over them, but the sparks rarely caught flame in my own heart. In retrospect, I think it was because no one ever taught me to name sin for myself. Instead, they spent their time naming it for me, as it related to their lives, not mine.

As I said earlier, there are numerous reasons why the language of sin and salvation has lost power in recent decades. In its stead, several other languages have emerged to describe the human predicament. The two most influential—the languages of medicine and law—have been embraced both by the church and the culture.

In the medical model, the basic human problem is not called sin but sickness. Everyone is vulnerable to sickness and very few people avoid being sick at some time in their lives. Since no one in his or her right mind chooses to be sick, it does not make any sense to hold sick people responsible for their illnesses. A person with advanced Alzheimer's cannot decide to be lucid any more than a person with bipolar disorder can decide to stop having mood swings. Both persons have illnesses that restrict their freedom and limit their responsibility. To hold either of them accountable for their actions would be to blame the victims.

When sickness is substituted for sin, then illness becomes the metaphor for human failing. We receive diagnosis instead of judgment, treatment instead of penance. Sometimes our problems are caused by bacteria or biochemistry. Other times they can be traced back to traumatic childhood events. Either way, they cannot properly be called our "fault." We do what we do because of what has been done to us. Since we did not deform ourselves, we cannot re-form ourselves. What we need is a compassionate physician who is not repelled by our disease and who will never stop trying to heal us.

I hear this language used more in the tradition of liberal Christianity. It has biblical precedent, and lends itself to a kind of no-fault theology based on an existential understanding of sin as all-pervasive and unavoidable. We all do the best we can. If some of us do better than others, then that is because we were dealt a better hand to begin with. People hit children because they were hit themselves. People do destructive things because no one ever taught them how to value life, especially not their own.

Do you remember that great line from the old movie *Charade*, when Audrey Hepburn turns to Cary Grant and asks him, "Why do people lie?"

"People lie," he says, "because they want something and fear that the truth will not get it for them." If he had been a preacher instead of a movie star, he might have said, "People sin because they want something and fear that goodness will not get it for them."

This fear, this human weakness, is so common among us that we might as well call it *affliction* as sin. We all experience existential angst. Judgment hardly seems appropriate. Why would God condemn anyone for being weak or afraid?

The language of law heads in the opposite direction. In the legal model, the basic human problem is not called sin or sickness but crime. Whether the offense is as minor as running a stop sign or as major as shooting someone else in the head, the presence of laws prohibiting these behaviors suggests that they are governable. We are responsible for our actions. Regardless of our circumstances, we are free to avoid lives of crime, and we are furthermore expected to do so.

If we fail—and if we are caught—then we will have to face the consequences. These may range from fines to prison terms, depending on the offense. Submitting to this punishment is how we pay our debt to society. When the debt is paid, then we are restored to community (at least in theory), although our records remain on file. If we fail again, then the punishment will be harsher next time, and if we show no promise of improvement, then we may be removed from society altogether, by receiving either life without parole or the death penalty.

When crime is substituted for sin, then lawlessness becomes the metaphor for human failing. The answer is not medicine but a swift dose of justice. No matter how we grew up, no matter what kind of difficulties we may be having in the present, we are expected to abide by God's law, and, if we do not, to accept responsibility for our actions. We do what we do because we choose to, and if sin continues to dog our steps then that is because we are either careless or rebellious. What we need is a fair but righteous judge who will brush away our excuses and hold us accountable for our actions.

I hear this language used more in the tradition of conservative Christianity. It too has biblical precedent, and lends itself to a kind of full-fault theology based on an understanding of sin as willful misbehavior. The emphasis here is on the individual believer who has power to choose between good and evil. Situational ethics does not apply. There is right and there is wrong. Depending on which one you choose, you are either a stalk of wheat or a tare, a sheep or a goat, a wise maiden or foolish one. When the judge comes, he will reveal who is who and eternal sentences will be handed down. No small part of the appeal of this model is its belief that we can single out the wrongdoers and put them away, freeing those of us who have not been caught for anything to enjoy a bracing sense of innocence.

My concern is that neither the language of medicine nor the language of law is an adequate substitute for the language of theology, which has more room in it for paradox than either of the other two. In the theological model, the basic human problem is not sickness or lawlessness but sin. It is something we experience both as a species and as individuals, in our existential angst and in our willful misbehavior. However we run into it, we run into it as wrecked relationship: with God, with one another, with the whole created order. Sometimes we cause the wreckage and sometimes we are simply trapped in it, but either way we are not doomed.

Contrary to the medical model, we are not entirely at the mercy of our maladies. Even within a fallen creation, we still have pockets of God-given freedom. However impoverished our circumstances, however badly we may have been used, we may still choose—for good or ill—how we will respond to what has happened to us. We may learn how to live with our tragedies or we may spend all of our time dying from them. We may decide to forgive our enemies or we may allow them to run our lives by continuing to hate them. In theological language, the choice to remain in wrecked relationship with God and other human beings is called sin. The choice to enter into the process of repair is called repentance, an often bitter medicine with the undisputed power to save lives.

Contrary to the legal model, sin is not simply a set of behaviors to be avoided. Much more fundamentally, it is a way of life to be exposed and changed, and no one is innocent. But that fact need not paralyze anyone with fear, since the proper response to sin is not punishment but penance. I will speak more about the difference between the two later, but for now the point is that the essence of sin is not the violation of laws but the violation of relationships. Punishment is not paramount. Restoration of relationship is paramount, which means that the focus is not on paying debts but on recovering fullness of life.

Christian theology is neither no-fault nor full-fault. We do wrong, but we do not do wrong all alone. We live in a web of creation that binds us to all other living beings. If we want to be saved, then we had better figure out how to do it together, since none of us can resign from this web of relationship.

Meanwhile, sin is our only hope, because the recognition that something is wrong is the first step toward setting it right again. There is no help for those who admit no need of help. There is no repair for those who insist that nothing is broken, and there is no hope of transformation for a world whose inhabitants accept that it is sadly but irreversibly wrecked.

The wreckage scenario is a tempting one to accept. Every now and then someone does something truly heroic to help put things right. A Desmond Tutu dreams up a truth-telling project to begin setting the broken bones of his nation, or a Mother Teresa takes the dying outcasts of Calcutta into her arms and bathes them as she would bathe Christ himself, but not many of us see ourselves in their class. Where *do* people find the time to be heroic? It is all most of us can do to keep the house clean and the bills paid.

So we devote ourselves to those things, and to all the other urgent duties of keeping up in a fast-paced world. We compete, we achieve, we accumulate and defend. We see therapists who help us maintain our boundaries and manage our guilt. We tend to our own business and trust others to tend to theirs, all the while trying to convince ourselves that this growing ache inside—this sense of being cut off from what really matters—is normal. It is not a sign that something is wrong. It is just a pain to be gotten used to, like monthly cramps or hemorrhoids. Call it existential anxiety. Call it the human condition. Call it life.

If, on the other hand, you decide to call it sin, then you have already made a radical shift in your perception of reality. You have admitted that something is wrong, for one thing, and you have chosen a term that requires something of you—if not an outright confession of your peccability, then at least an admission of your frailty: that you are sick and tired of being sick and tired, that you cannot live with this suffocating ache one moment longer, that you are as ready as you will ever be for a whole new life. As hard as such a confession may be, it is also a confession of hope—that things may change, that the way they are is not the way they must always be. The catch, of course, is that this hope begins with some acceptance of your responsibility for the way things are.

If you have ever gotten to that point yourself, then you know how easy it is to glow like a furnace for a couple of days and then to gradually cool off until everything is back to what passes for "normal." Often it is the people you love most who will try hardest to pat you back down into place.

"Honey, I know you think you want to quit your job and spend more time with the kids, but we can't stay in this house without two incomes. Why don't you give it six months and see if you still feel the same way in September?"

"Drink too much? I don't think you drink too much. I think you just know how to have a good time without looking down your nose at people. If you want to cut back, then go right ahead, but quit? What would we do on weekends if you quit? Who would our friends be?"

Some of you know the writer Reynolds Price, who suffered from a rare form of spinal cancer in the mid-eighties and lost the use of his legs. His crisis was not only physical but also spiritual, since his illness required him to change his entire way of life. What surprised him most, he said, was the resistance of his friends.

"When we undergo huge traumas in middle life," he said, "everybody is in league with us to deny that the old life is ended. Everybody is trying to patch us up and get us back to who we were, when in fact what we need to be told is, 'You're dead. Who are you going to be tomorrow?'"[5]

The recognition of sin in our lives constitutes one such trauma. To measure the full distance between where we are and where God created us to be—to suffer that distance, to name it, to decide not to live quietly with it any longer—that is the moment when we know we are dead and begin to decide who we will be tomorrow.

When I say "sin," there is no telling what you see: the stolen candy bar, the rumpled sheets of a bed you shared with someone else's lover, a large pipe spilling orange sludge into a once-blue river, a clutch of homeless people sitting around a fire built from trash in a vacant lot between two corporate skyscrapers. The picture will be different for every one of you, but the experience to hunt for is that one that makes part of you die.

Deep down in human existence, there is an experience of being cut off from life. There is some memory of having been treated cruelly, and—a little deeper, perhaps—the memory of having treated someone else cruelly as well. Deep down in human existence there is an experience of seeing the light and turning away from it, either because it is too beautiful to behold or because it spoils the dank but familiar darkness. Deep down in human existence there is an experience of reaching for forbidden fruit, of pushing away loving arms, of breaking something on purpose just to prove that you can. Deep down in human existence there is an experience of doing whatever is necessary to feed and comfort the self, because there is no one else to trust, no other purpose to serve, no other god to follow.

For ages and ages, this experience has been called sin—deadly alienation from the source of all life. By some definitions, it implies willful turning away from God. By others, it is an unavoidable feature of being human. Either way, it is a name for the experience of being cut off from air, light, sustenance, community, hope, meaning, *life*. It is less concerned with specific behaviors than with the aftermath of those behaviors. There are a thousand ways to turn away from the light, after all, with variations according to culture, century, class, and gender. The point is to know the difference between light and darkness, and to recognize the pull of darkness when it comes.

Several years ago I was in a preaching workshop with a woman who said that every time she stood up in front of her congregation to speak, her stomach began to cramp. Sometimes the pain would increase to the point that she was forced to bring her sermon hurriedly to an end. Upon hearing this, another woman in the group said the most surprising thing. "It's sin!" she announced. "There has to be sin in there somewhere, if it is tearing your stomach up like that."

Because this diagnostician had already established herself as a trustworthy person, we dared to explore her insight. As it turned out, the woman with the stomach problem had deep doubts about her worthiness as a preacher. She had grown up in a household where little girls' voices did not count for much, and her eventual decision to go to seminary had met with her family's disapproval. She furthermore had an "enemy" in the congregation, a woman around her age who consistently made cutting remarks about her sermons.

She had never thought about her problem in terms of sin, she said, since she had always heard sin defined as self-aggrandizement. In our group that day, we discovered another definition of sin as self-negation. As different as the two definitions are, their aftermath is the same: a refusal of one's God-given place in community, with a resultant loss of life and health.

When we widen the lens, we can see this aftermath in our national life as well. While America still looks strong on the outside, anyone who lives here knows that we have some gut problems too. We live in the richest, most powerful country on earth. We police other nations without their consent, and employ their workers for a fraction of what we would pay our own. We are not always welcome when we travel abroad. We throw away more food each year than some small nations produce, and we have no rivals in terms of our despoilment of the earth. "We all live by robbing nature," writes the farmer-poet Wendell Berry, "But our standard of living demands that the robbery shall continue."[6]

While most Americans continue to cherish the illusion that we live in a classless, equal-opportunity society, our courts, our prisons, our public assistance programs, and our schools all tell a different story. It is difficult to believe that we are still debating whether hate crimes are really crimes, and whether guns really kill people. Meanwhile, our technological achievements serve not only to make the rich richer but also to make sure the poor will remain poorer. A first grader who does not have a computer at home will struggle to keep up with classmates who do. Computers may soon rival automobiles as the possessions most necessary for survival in America—a prospect that cheers stockholders' hearts, and increases the despair of those who live below the poverty line. At last count, Bill Gates' personal fortune equaled the assets of 43 percent of the American people combined.

Meanwhile, new technology has real consequences for the earth—not only the obvious things going on in the sky and in the water table, but also the more invisible things going on at the dump, where outdated computers, copiers, record players, VCRs and telephone systems form a new genre of trash. In the face of realities like these, sexual transgressions and violation of church laws do not seem to be the sins that should most concern us at this time. Instead, the ways that we earn, spend, and invest our money may have more sin in them than anything else we do.

Repentance begins with the decision to return to relationship: to accept our God-given place in community, and to choose a way of life that increases life for all members of that community. Needless to say, this often involves painful changes, which is why most of us prefer remorse to repentance. We would rather say, "I'm sorry, I'm so sorry, I feel really, really awful about what I have done" than actually start doing things differently. As a wise counselor once pointed out to me, our chronic guilt is the price we are willing to pay in order to avoid change. We believe that if we feel badly enough about what we are doing, then we may continue doing it. Plus, the guilt itself is so exhausting that it drives us right back into the arms of our sins, which may provide us with our only reliable comfort.

"All sins are attempts to fill voids," wrote the French philosopher Simone Weil. Because we cannot stand the God-shaped hole inside of us, we try stuffing it full of all sorts of things, but it refuses to be filled. It rejects all substitutes. It insists on remaining bare. It is the holy of holies inside of us, which only God may fill.

When we are ready to honor the bare space instead of trying to stuff it full, then we are ready to consider what kind of new life God may be calling us to. Our answers will be as varied as our sins, but they will involve more doing than saying, more reformation than remorse. Meanwhile, I do not believe that sin is the enemy we often make it out to be, at least not when we recognize it and name it as such. When we see how we have turned away from God, then and only then do we have what we need to begin turning back. Sin is our only hope, the fire alarm that wakes us up to the possibility of true repentance.

Three

Recovering Repentance

—

WHILE THE PUBLIC CONFESSION OF SIN IS A REGU-lar feature of most Christian worship, ancient tradition provides for heightened penitence during the season of Lent. The word comes from the old English word for "spring," a refer-ence not only to what is happening in the natural world but also to what is happening in the spiritual world. Lent covers the six weeks before Easter, the great Christian festival of new life, when the hard, buried bulbs of our souls come into full flower.

As any good gardener knows, new life requires some assis-tance. The life itself is entirely God's gift, but the cultivation of it calls for work. There is some tilling and fertilizing to be done, some weeding and pruning of dead branches. Without such in-tentional participation in the renewal of life, the roses will even-tually disappear under the poke-weed, and the Japanese beetles will eat all of the peaches.

For earlier Christians, the season of Lent was set aside for the greening of the soul, which began with penitence and fast-ing. New converts were prepared for holy baptism on Easter eve, and people whose sins had separated them from the community were invited back. Those who decided to accept the invitation knew that more would be required of them than simply showing up. During Lent, they would join the whole congregation in the solemn work of self-examination and repentance, designed to renew their faith in God and restore their fellowship with one another.

The season begins forty days before Easter on a Wednesday—Ash Wednesday—which gets its name from a church service that includes the imposition of ashes. Early in the liturgy, the congregation is invited forward to kneel at the altar rail. Then the clergy go from person to person, dipping their thumbs into small bowls of ashes and making the sign of the cross on each forehead. "Remember that you are dust," they say, "and to dust you shall return" (BCP 265).

Any way they say it, this is fairly sobering language. It is hard enough for a healthy adult to hear, but when it is said to a three-year-old child, or a person gaunt from chemotherapy, it can sound too harsh for words. It is language that yanks away all our deceit about death. Our eventual demise is no longer theory but fact. Whatever pretty pictures we have painted for the stage sets of our lives, Ash Wednesday parts the curtains so that we can see the brick wall behind. It is the same brick wall for every one of us, which unites us even as it makes our throats go dry. We all came from dust, and to dust we shall all return.

For those who have been baptized, there is some comfort in knowing that the ash cross goes on top of an earlier cross made from water. The promise of new life underlies the reminder of death, which is where we find the courage to go on with the Ash Wednesday service. Psalm 51 comes next ("Have mercy on me, O God"), and after that the Litany of Penitence, in which we confess not only our own sins but also the sins of the whole world.

Entering more than a dozen guilty pleas, we confess our lack of love for our neighbors, along with our deafness to God's call to serve. We confess our self-indulgent appetites and ways, our envy of those more fortunate than ourselves, and our negligence

in prayer and worship. Then we ask God to believe that we mean
to change.

> Accept our repentance, Lord, for the wrongs we have
> done: for our blindness to human need and suffering,
> and our indifference to injustice and cruelty,
> *Accept our repentance, Lord.*

> For all false judgments, for uncharitable thoughts toward
> our neighbors, and for our prejudice and contempt
> toward those who differ from us,
> *Accept our repentance, Lord.*

> For our waste and pollution of your creation, and our
> lack of concern for those who come after us,
> *Accept our repentance, Lord.*

> Restore us, good Lord, and let your anger depart from us;
> *Favorably hear us, for your mercy is great.*

> Accomplish in us the work of your salvation,
> *That we may show forth your glory in the world.*

> By the cross and passion of your Son our Lord,
> *Bring us with all your saints to the joy of his resurrection.*
> (BCP 268)

Then the celebrant makes the sign of the cross over us, reminding us that God pardons and absolves all those who truly
repent, and who with sincere hearts believe the holy gospel. After
the service is over, most of us stumble out the door of the church
and walk blinking back into the world where we have jobs to do

and errands to run. For the rest of the day people will look quizzically at our faces, and a few will helpfully tell us that we have dirt on our foreheads. Although I have never actually done it, I have been tempted to say, "Yes, I know. That's my mortality. I thought I'd let it show today."

I think it is safe to say that Christians need never fear the commercialization of Ash Wednesday. Hallmark will never spend much money on research and design, and shopkeepers will not dress their windows in sackcloth and ashes. There is no apparent danger that repentance will ever catch on with the culture at large, especially since it does not sell all that well in church.

After last year's Ash Wednesday service was over, I did some shopping, went to a meeting, drove home, and cooked supper. While I was doing all of that I wondered what my noontime repentance was really worth. I had repented of my blindness to human need and suffering, but I still drove past the homeless man at the intersection with my window rolled up. I had repented of my contempt toward those who differ from me, but I still thought mean things about the people in the meeting whose votes cancelled mine. I had repented of my waste and pollution of God's creation, but that did not stop me from buying a new Hewlett-Packard Office Jet printer so that my old Panasonic could end up on a junk heap somewhere. You see the problem.

I am not sure what the word "repentance" means anymore. Words without actions do not seem very meaningful to me, and individual good intentions without community support to back them up seem doomed to fail. There is something powerful about kneeling with other people and saying true things about our failure to live up to God's high call, but if all we do when it is over is climb in our cars and go our separate ways, then I wonder if God really cares.

Several years ago, I decided to try and bridge this gap. I asked another woman to enter into a support partnership with me, and together we designed a routine. After deciding to start small, each of us chose one area of our lives that needed work. We clarified what we wanted to change (I wanted to be on time for my appointments) and we clarified why it was important (I wanted to be a person of my word, and I also wanted to do something about my compulsion to cram too many things into too little time, which is how I act out my idolatrous fantasy of omnipotence). Next we picked one or two specific actions that would support us to make the changes we wanted to make (I will set all my clocks five minutes ahead. I will also get in the car ten minutes earlier than I think I need to, even if it means that I arrive early and—gasp—*waste time*). Finally, we agreed to call each other every Sunday to report on how things were going.

This last step turned out to be the kicker. There was a huge difference between saying (to myself), "I want to be on time for my appointments this week" and saying (to someone else), "I will call you on Sunday to tell you whether or not I was." My partner never badgered me. She knew that was not her job. Her job was simply to keep reminding me what I had said I wanted, and to help me explore my enormous resistance to change.

What I learned through that process was that I was used to being sympathized with for my failure to change. There were plenty of people I could talk to about being late who would say, "Oh, I'm late all the time too. Isn't it awful?" I was also used to being punished for my failure to change. At least one person I pushed to the edge finally said, "I get so tired of waiting for you to show up that sometimes I forget why I wanted to see you at all." What I was *not* used to was being supported in my bid for new life by someone who said, "You want to do things differently? Great! I'll help you with that." When all was said and done, it was easier for me to receive sympathy or punishment from other people than it was to let one other person uphold me in the hard work of transformation.

To return to the medical and legal paradigms I introduced earlier, I think that I can see this same kind of thing going on in the church. It is easy for me to think of churches that operate like clinics, where sin-sick patients receive sympathetic care for the disease they all share. It is palliative care, for the most part. No one expects anyone to be fully cured, which is why there is not much emphasis on individual sin. Such churches subscribe to a kind of no-fault theology in which no one is responsible because everyone is.

It is also easy for me to think of churches that operate like courts, where both sins and sinners are named out loud, along with punishments appropriate to their crimes. On the whole, the sinners identified by this full-fault theology tend to be people who do not belong to the fold, but I do know of one church that calls pregnant, unmarried teenagers up before the congregation to be publicly rebuked.

True repentance will not serve either of these purposes. It will not work in the church-as-clinic because repentance will not make peace with sin. Instead, it calls individuals to take responsibility for what is wrong with the world—beginning with what is wrong with them—and to join with other people who are dedicated to turning things around. True repentance will not work in the church-as-courtroom either, because it is not interested in singling out scapegoats and punishing them. Instead, it calls whole communities to engage in the work of repair and reconciliation without ever forgetting their own culpability for the way things are. If individual sinners are called to account, then it is never for the purpose of harming or humiliating them, but always with the goal of restoring them to life.

Bent as we are either on excusing sin or pounding it into the ground, it is no wonder that a third kind of church is so hard to find—not church-as-clinic nor church-as-courtroom, but church-as-community-of-transformation, where members are expected and supported to be about the business of new life.

Since I have very limited experience of such churches, I cannot tell you much about them. Last year I visited the Church of the Savior in Washington, D.C., a community dedicated to change in the name of Jesus Christ. Begun fifty years ago by founding pastor Gordon Cosby, the church's efforts are focused on the Adams Morgan neighborhood in Washington, where low income Ethiopian, Latino, and Anglo families have all settled in uneasy proximity to one another.

Unlike traditional churches, the Church of the Savior is a collection of independent faith communities, all dedicated to restoring wholeness to people with broken lives. Each community has evolved its own mission group, and the fruits of their labors are evident in a short drive through the neighborhood. Columbia Road Health Services provides affordable health care for anyone who needs it. Christ House is a medical recovery residence for homeless people, and Kairos House is a permanent home for thirty-seven chronically ill homeless men who are not going to get better, in this life at least.

The Family Place offers prenatal and pediatric care as well as a whole range of services for families, and Good Shepherd Ministries provides educational and recreational programs for more than a hundred children and adolescents. Samaritan Inns helps addicted men and women rebuild their lives, and Jubilee Housing rents 284 apartments in eight buildings to low income families at less than 40 percent of market. Jubilee Jobs is an employment agency for the poor, and Sarah's Circle is a residential community for the elderly.

Repentance may not be the first word that comes to your

mind when you see this remarkable array, but these ministries are all founded on a vision of ending the estrangement between rich and poor—an estrangement that is as full of sin as any other in our culture. The Church of the Savior is very clear that it does not do charity work. The Church of the Savior is working to break down the dividing wall between the privileged and the deprived, so that each may recognize God in the other.

Elizabeth O'Connor, who was a rock of the community until her recent death, said that when she walked the streets of Adams Morgan she often caught a glimpse of the new Jerusalem coming out of the skies. In a church brochure, she wrote:

> On these streets are spoken the tongues of many lands and still we understand what people are saying. Here some of the refugees of the world have found a safe place to lay their heads, cradle their babies, and sell their wares from folding tables and tiny stores. Here the demented can still wander in and out of our shops. Here some places have been made for the young and the old. Here the broken are received and the sick healed. Here the Gospel is being preached and here, faulted as we are, with our own griefs heavily upon us, we are bold to say that God calls us his people and we know that his name is God-with-them.[7]

On a much more modest scale, I recently visited an Alcoholics Anonymous group that meets in the basement of a small Presbyterian church. I was there at the invitation of a young man who was celebrating his second year of sobriety. Two years earlier, he almost died when he wrecked his car while he was driving under the influence of drugs and alcohol. Luckily for him, his sentence included a rehabilitation program and a long period of parole during which he became an active member of AA.

The night I was there, his parents were, too, along with his younger brother. For one hour we all sat in a room with people who were dedicated to the work of transformation. The young man spoke frankly about his self-destructiveness, his former deception of his friends and family, and the strong temptation he sometimes felt to go back to the way things were. The other people in the room nodded knowingly. A few even reminded him of some sordid things he had done that he had left out of his narrative. More than once, I wanted to jump up and clap my hands over his mother's ears—not because anyone was saying anything mean about her or her son, but simply because they were speaking the truth in her presence.

She was fine with it. My own response taught me that for all my conscious belief in the transforming power of the truth I still have an unconscious fear of it, even when it is told in a protected setting with the full consent of all present. What am I afraid of? That someone will be revealed for who he or she is. That I will be revealed for who I am, and that it will not be a pretty sight.

And yet the people in that room believe that their lives depend on doing exactly that—revealing themselves to one another—and furthermore allowing one another to say what they see when they do. If you are an AA member yourself, then you know that is one of the reasons you keep going back: because there are so few places in the world where people agree to tell the truth like that, and where that truth works the miracle of change.

What struck me, both in Washington and in the Presbyterian church basement, was the absence of self-defense. In neither place did I hear people blaming anything on anyone else or talking about how change was impossible for them until someone else changed. Whether the challenge was a rough neighborhood in the murder capital of the world, or one roomful of people wrestling the demon of addiction, the assumption was that new life was possible, and that everyone present was responsible for bringing it about.

The reality of that new life and the promise that it is reachable are both contained in the word salvation. The root word is *salus*, or health, which points back toward the medical paradigm, except that this health plan is truly comprehensive. Physical health cannot be separated from mental and spiritual health, nor individual health from the health of the whole—the whole community, the whole race, the whole earth. In Hebrew scripture, salvation comes as the gift of *shalom* from Yahweh, who intends to heal the whole creation. In Christianity, salvation comes in the person of Jesus Christ, who intends the same thing.

One mistake many of us have made is to use the word as if it meant intellectual assent to a particular set of beliefs. Or, as it was explained to me at my own conversion almost thirty years ago, salvation means accepting the Lordship of Christ. With all due respect, I am not sure that Jesus would agree. Jesus saves, but not by alchemy. Some response on our part is required. Based on my reading of scripture, it seems entirely possible that Jesus might define salvation as recovery from illness or addiction, as forgiveness of debt, as peace between old enemies, as shared food in time of famine, or as justice for the poor. These are all outbreaks of health in a sin-sick world. Jesus saves because he shows us how to multiply such outbreaks, and because he continues to be present in them. Otherwise, we might call them good works or good luck. Instead, we have this sense that they come to us from outside of us. Our full participation is required, but that alone cannot explain the results, which are sometimes so astounding that we can only call them grace.

One question worth asking is what moves us to seek salvation. What moves us to repent? There are as many answers to that question as there are readers of this book, but I do believe that each age has its own peculiar hell. The things that frighten us now are not the things that frightened our forebears, and the fears of Chinese Christians are different from the fears of Christians living in Kenya. The gospel may remain the same wherever it is proclaimed, but the people who hear it are not the same. Our ears are conditioned by the cultures in which we have learned to speak, hear, live, and make sense of our lives.

Douglas John Hall is a Canadian theologian who has spent his life thinking about what Christianity means in a North American context. Focusing specifically on the Christianity of the United States and Canada, Hall suggests that we are not motivated by the same fears other Christians are, nor even the same fears our ancestors were. Death, for instance, does not scare us as much as it did a thousand years ago, when life expectancy hovered around forty and the only social safety net was the family. Nor does the threat of damnation work as well as it did even a hundred years ago, when Christendom still had clout. Instead, Hall suggests, what eats away at us is the gnawing suspicion that we may be superfluous—an accidental species with no real purpose on earth.[8]

When people feel superfluous, Hall says—when we are deprived of meaningful work, meaningful relationships, meaningful goals—when we cannot find a purpose big enough for our capabilities, then we frequently become destructive. Our destructiveness may be focused outward, resulting in crime and violence, or it may be focused inward, resulting in depression and addiction. Either way, the threat of meaninglessness is our primary motive for repentance, and salvation comes as we discover (or rediscover) purpose for our lives.

This description may sound too abstract for people who want to be told what they should and should not do, but it honors Tillich's advice about how to revive the lost, great words of our tradition. It is not enough for us to try and understand what they once meant. If we want the language to come alive again, then we will plunge back into the depths of human existence, where the words were first conceived and where they may once again be filled with power. It is work no generation can do for another, nor one individual for another. The church's job—and the preacher's job within the church—is to evoke the depths so vividly that sparks jump between the words and the realities they describe.

To use Hall's language, the church exists so that God has a community in which to save people from meaninglessness, by reminding them who they are and what they are for. The church exists so that God has a place to point people toward a purpose as big as their capabilities, and to help them identify all the ways they flee from that high call. The church exists so that people have a community in which they may confess their sin—their own turning away from life, whatever form that destructiveness may take for them—as well as a community that will support them to turn back again. The church exists so that people have a place where they may repent of their fear, their hardness of heart, their isolation and loss of vision, and where—having repented—they may be restored to fullness of life.

In a life of faith so conceived, God's grace is not simply the infinite supply of divine forgiveness upon which hopeless sinners depend. Grace is also the mysterious strength God lends human beings who commit themselves to the work of transformation. To repent is both to act from that grace and to ask for more of it, in order to follow Christ into the startling freedom of new life.

I remember a classmate of mine, a Lebanese Presbyterian, who threw a theological temper tantrum during his first semester in seminary. "All you Americans care about is justification!" he howled. "You love sinning and being forgiven, sinning and being forgiven, but no one seems to want off that hamster wheel. Have you ever heard of sanctification? Is anyone interested in learning to sin a little less?"

Traditionally, the way off the hamster wheel has had at least four steps to it: confession, pardon, penance, and restoration to community. The real mystery, of course, is what moves a person or a group of people to change in the first place. What happens inside a person to make him choose life without the anesthesia of alcohol or cocaine? What happens inside a community to make them choose downward mobility, instead of up? This mysterious freedom and willingness to choose is both the beginning and end of repentance, which I can only explain as God's gift. By restoring our freedom to choose, God restores the divine image in us. We are not only shown the difference between the way of life and the way of death; we are also granted the power to choose life.

This choosing usually begins with the confession that something is or has been wrong. In the New Testament, confessions tend to be public. John's baptisms all involve the confession of sin. The letter of James suggests that community confession was a prerequisite for healing the sick (5:16). In the nineteenth chapter of the book of Acts, you can read about a fairly spectacular public confession that happened during Paul's tenure in Ephesus. "Many of those who became believers confessed and disclosed their practices," it reads. "A number of those who practiced magic collected their books and burned them publicly; when the value of these books was calculated, it was found to come to fifty thousand silver coins. So the word of the Lord grew mightily and prevailed" (19:18-20).

While most of us would prefer to disclose our practices privately, our reluctance to be overheard tells us everything we need to know about the power of community. Once one other person knows about our sins, they are no longer secret. We can no longer deny their existence, nor rearrange the details so that someone else seems to be at fault. When we confess our sins in community, we admit witnesses into our lives. We consent to be known by them and we ask for their help.

This radical act of self-disclosure has a way of transforming the confessor as well as the confessee. I have already told you how I saw it work in an AA meeting. For an example of how confession works on a larger scale, consider the Truth and Reconciliation Commission of South Africa. By the time apartheid officially ended in 1990, black and white South Africans had several ways to proceed. They could each try to throw the other out of the country through terrorism or outright revolution. They could use the laws that were in place to prosecute one another. Or they could seek peace.

In most places, as you know, peace means little more than cessation of hostilities. Each side agrees to stop waging war on the other, but transforming their relationship with one another is not usually part of the agenda. In South Africa, however, a larger vision took hold. Under the leadership of Desmond Tutu, with the strong backing of the South Africa Council of Churches, the Truth and Reconciliation Commission was set up as a way that might allow former enemies to live together in peace.

That way has involved people from both sides standing up in front of other people and confessing the horrible things they have done. White policemen have confessed to slamming drawers on the breasts of black women prisoners until the women said whatever the policemen wanted them to say. Black protestors have confessed to killing innocent people for the crime of having white skin. What is more, all of these sinners have confessed their sins in the presence of their victims' families, so that they can see on those people's faces the full impact of what they have done. The hope embedded in this process is a simple one: that truth has power to set people free.

In the classical scheme, pardon comes next—before any repa-
rations have been made, before lives show any long-term evidence
of change—pardon comes next, because without it we might not
have enough hope to engage the work of transformation. The
arduous journey to restoration is yet to come, but pardon is our
promise that there will be somewhere for us to stay when we arrive. While the pardon may be pronounced by human beings, it
always comes from God, since God is the only one who is really
very good at forgiveness. The word can sound a little hollow in
the rest of our mouths.

"I forgive you, but I will never trust you again."

"I forgive you, but I don't want to see you anymore." What is
forgiveness without reunion, or at least the possibility of reunion?

And yet there are consequences to our actions. I was fasci-
nated to speak with a Hindu colleague of mine about the concept
of karma in her faith. "Every human choice has moral fallout," she
explained. "If you harm me, then there will be consequences for
you as well as for me. You may have a change of heart later and
ask me to forgive you, but even if I forgive you from the bottom
of my heart, I cannot change your karma. You made a choice,
which has had its effect. Eventually, you, too, will experience its
full effect."

This is a scary idea for some Christians, who like to think of
forgiveness as a giant eraser on the blackboard of life. But there is
biblical precedent for the lasting effects of sins that have been forgiven. God forgave David for his murderous affair with Bathsheba,
but their firstborn child still died. Jesus came to forgive the sins of
the whole world, but according to his parable in Matthew 25, he
will come again to separate the sheep from the goats.

Forgiveness is a starting place, not a stopping place. It is God's
gift to those who wish to begin again, but where we go with it is
up to us. As I said earlier, most of us prefer remorse to repentance.

We would rather feel badly about the damage we have done than get estimates on the cost of repair. We would rather learn to live with guilt than face the hard work of new life.

While penance has all but disappeared from our vocabulary, it was once the church's best tool for getting over that hump. Once a person had confessed her sins and received assurance of pardon, she voluntarily took on specific acts of penance, which were baby steps in the direction of new life. If she had stolen vegetables from a neighbor's garden, then she might volunteer to weed the garden every other day for a month. If she had slandered someone, then she might revisit all the households where she had done that and set the record straight.

Penance was not punishment. Penance was repair. Penance was a way back into relationship, but like all other good spiritual practices, it was vulnerable to corruption. In some places it became routine and trivialized. In others it became a means of extortion. When the Protestant reformers rebelled against certain aspects of Catholic theology and practice, penance was one of the babies that was thrown out with the bath water. It smacked of works righteousness, the reformers said. It was ripe for abuse. It undercut grace.

One consequence of its disappearance, however, is that we have lost this very powerful way of living into our repentance. As a result, many of us have learned to substitute words for actions. We say that we are sorry for our faults. Jesus says that he forgives us, and that is supposed to be that. Bygones are supposed to be bygones, but you know it is not true.

As admirable as South Africa's efforts at national repentance have been, it now appears that confession and pardon alone are not enough. When Lucas Sekwepere testified before the Truth and Reconciliation Commission in 1996, he told them how he had been shot in the face by a white policeman ten years earlier.

After he was blinded, he said, he was tortured for information. One night his captors put a bag over his head, twisting it tighter and tighter until he was sure he would suffocate. Another night they led him to a cemetery, where they dropped him in an open grave and threatened to bury him alive. Asked how he felt about testifying, he said, "I feel what has been making me sick all the time is the fact that I couldn't tell my story. But now it feels like I got my sight back, by coming here and telling you the story."

Four years later, he continues to live in darkness. After he testified, he understood that a doctor would examine him, if only to remove the bullet fragments still embedded in his face. He expected he might receive job training so that he could work. He hoped to hear of some change in his squalid neighborhood once apartheid had ended, but so far the only reparation he has received is a government check for $700. "Not much," he says, "for someone who has been hungry for fifteen years."

Meanwhile, more than six hundred perpetrators have been granted amnesty in South Africa. Full disclosure is all the commission required of them. Once they had publicly confessed their sins, they were free to go. Two years after the conclusion of the hearings, more and more victims are doubting that there can be any lasting peace without justice. Unless those who suffered see real material transformation in their lives, warns Tutu, "you can kiss reconciliation goodbye."[9]

To translate that into the terms I have been using, repentance is not complete until confession and pardon lead to penance that allows community to be restored. Archbishop Tutu's insistence on real material transformation is not a surrender of spiritual values. Instead, it is evidence of his faith in Christ's incarnation, which shows us how much flesh and blood matter to God. Salvation is not offered to us as some kind of metaphysical prize. It is offered to us in our bodies as God's manifest power to change human lives. While Jesus may have done the hardest work for us, some of us still long for a way both to engage the consequences of our sin and to have a hand in repairing the damage we have done. We want to participate in our own redemption, instead of sitting in a lawn chair while Jesus does all the work. We want to be agents of God's grace.

Just for a lark, imagine going to your pastor and confessing your rampant materialism, your devotion to things instead of people, and your isolation from the poor whom Jesus loved. Then imagine being forgiven and given your penance: to select five of your favorite things—including perhaps your Bose radio and your new Coach book bag—and to match them up with five people who you know would turn cartwheels to have them. Then on Saturday, put your lawn mower in your trunk, drive down to that transitional neighborhood where all the old people live and offer to mow lawns for free until dark. Discerning sinners will note that none of this is standard punishment. It is penance, which is not for the purpose of inflicting pain but for the much higher purpose of changing lives by restoring relationships.

Something like that might really get my attention. I might begin to understand that repentance means more than saying "I'm sorry" and that God's grace requires more of me than singing every verse of "Just As I Am."

It is interesting, by the way, that some people in the criminal justice system are beginning to consider this more theological approach to corrections. In the fall of 1999, over 250 church leaders, criminal justice employees, politicians, and service providers gathered at the National Cathedral in Washington, D.C., for the first national conference on restorative justice. Criminal justice traditionally asks, "Who did it? What law did he break? How are we going to punish him?" Restorative justice asks, "What harm was done? What is needed to repair the harm? Who is responsible for repairing it?"

Penance is the acceptance of responsibility for repair, and it is one of the most healing things a repentant sinner can do, as well as one of the most painful. While it may look like our own work, I do not think it is. Like the wake-up call to confession and the pardon that is offered, penance, too, is God's gift—as we find strength and courage we know we do not have to take measurable steps in the direction of new life.

That life is its own reward, but true repentance promises us more. It promises us reunion with God and one another. It promises us restoration to community, and to all the responsibilities that go along with life in relationship. Some of our old communities will not take us back, as many of you have discovered. That is simply part of the karma of sin. But God's pardon, which we received so long ago, carried with it the promise of new community—not stainless steel Christians who never bend or break, but a community of repentant sinners who know that the work of transformation is never done. Do you remember how Elizabeth O'Connor put it?

> Here the broken are received and the sick healed. Here
> the Gospel is being preached and here, faulted as we
> are, with our own griefs upon us, we are bold to say that
> God calls us his people and we know that his name is
> God-with-them.

I do not believe that there is any adequate substitute for this language. But in order to keep it alive, each of us must do our work—not only the work of diving down deep into human experience to find the realities the words describe, but also the work of bringing those words to life by clothing them in our own flesh. There is no reason why anyone should ever believe our talk of God's transforming power unless they can also see that transformation taking place in us—and through us, in the world. We are the people God has chosen to embody the gospel. Our lives are God's sign language in a sin-sick world, and God has promised us the grace we need to point the way home.

Postlude

Righteousness Redeemed

⟶

S EVERAL YEARS AGO I RECEIVED A TELEPHONE CALL from a man I went to college with. We had not spoken in twenty years, but somehow he heard that I had become an Episcopal priest and he wanted some advice. His best friends, who were also Episcopal, had just had a baby. They wanted him to stand with them at the boy's baptism and become their child's godfather, but as a Jew he wondered if he could.

We had never spoken of such things in college. I was barely Christian then and barely aware of his Jewishness. Twenty years later, our conversation was so warm that I was sorry we had lost track of one another. We talked about faith and barriers to faith. We talked about the similarities between our religions and the things that made them different. He said that he had some think-ing to do before he decided about the baptism. Then he thanked me for talking to him. "I can tell that you are a righteous person," he said, and hung up.

It was the most unusual compliment I had ever received. As a Christian, I had never heard the word "righteous" used positively in an ordinary conversation. All of my associations were negative, based on the derision with which I had heard "self-righteousness" and "works-righteousness" so often spoken. Wasn't righteousness what people relied on when they did not have faith? Clearly, my long lost college classmate knew the word from another context, which allowed him to use it in another way.

I spent days with the word after that, trying to figure out why mainline Christianity had abandoned it. The root word in Hebrew is *sadiq*, or justice. A righteous person is a just person, who reflects God's own righteousness by following God's commands. Since those commands are all about how to live in right relationship with God and one another, a righteous person's energies are directed entirely outward, toward others. Righteousness is relational. In every possible relationship, a righteous person lives as God wants—or means to live as God wants. Biblically speaking, the active desire for righteousness is as honorable as the fulfillment of it. The point is to seek God and the kind of life God intends.

Even now, it is very difficult for me to hear the compliment. I have been so schooled in Paul's theology that "righteous" still sounds like the opposite of "faithful" to me. He uses some form of the word (in Greek, *dike*) more than sixty times in his letter to the Romans, making a forensic distinction between the righteousness people may claim for themselves and the righteousness that only God can give, based on faith in Jesus Christ.

The problem is that two different English words are used to translate Paul's Greek. Sometimes the word comes through as "justification," which most of us associate with the phrase "by faith." Other times the word comes through as "righteousness," which just as many of us associate with "works." Both translations come from a single biblical concept—namely, that all righteousness/justification comes from God, is sustained by faith, and finds its fulfillment in a life distinguished by good works (or fruits of the spirit, if that language is easier on your ears).

Paul did not have anything against good works, as far as I can tell. He just did not want anyone getting the chicken confused with the egg. The golden egg of good works does not win anyone access to God. Instead, the egg is God's free prize to all who wish to hatch the gift of new life. Meanwhile, righteousness is essential to the process. Paul is famous for his long lists of how Christians are supposed to behave. Once a person has decided to follow Christ, then there is no longer any excuse for greed, gluttony, debauchery, deception, dissension, or litigation (among many other things). Righteousness arrives as God's gift and survives as God's requirement.

According to Matthew, those who hunger and thirst for it are blessed (5:6). Jesus expects the righteousness of his disciples to exceed that of the scribes and Pharisees (5:20). He himself is God's righteousness in the flesh (3:15). In him, it is possible to see what right relationship with God and neighbor looks like. It looks like justice. It looks like compassion. It looks like life lived in a covenant of ferocious, saving love.

I want this word back in my vocabulary. Much more importantly, I want the reality it names to be recovered by a church that has too often presented faith and works as opponents instead of partners in the divine paradox of grace. The great reformers never lost the paradox, but somewhere along the way their message has been flattened, so that it comes out something like this: All God cares about is whether or not we believe in Jesus. Once our faith has been established, any violence we do to one another in our battles of belief is justified, and any mistakes we make in the flesh are forgiven. All that matters to God is the inner disposition of our hearts.

When I look at the mischief that kind of theology has produced, I understand the midrash that quotes God as saying, "Would that they would forsake me, but obey my Torah."

One of the Hebrew words for a righteous person suggests

"one whose aim is true." Set beside the word that defines sin as "missing a mark," this gives me an image of righteousness as target practice. Whether my arrow finds its marks or falls a hundred feet away, the daily practice of right relationship is how I improve my aim. I will continue to sin, no doubt about it, but that is not my aim. My true aim is to live as God wants me to live and—as Thomas Merton once wrote—I believe that the wish to please God does in fact please God.

Since I sew more than I shoot arrows, I cannot help but extend the image. It is a needle I am wielding on my way through the world, with a sturdy brown thread looped through the silver eye. By the grace of God, I am being mended, and God has called me to be a mender too. Since many threads are stronger than one, God has put me on a sewing team. Day by day, our job is to hunt the places where the world is ripped and bend over the damage to do what we can. Every good deed, every kind word, every act of justice and compassion tugs the torn edges closer together. The truer our aim, the smaller our stitches and the longer the patch will hold. We made plenty of the rips ourselves, and some of the worst ones show evidence of having been mended many times before, but that does not seem to discourage anyone.

Mending is how we continue to be mended, and we would not trade the work for anything.

Endnotes

1. *The Book of Common Prayer*, hereafter *BCP*, 331.

2. Lewis H. Lapham, "Notebook: Asset Management," *Harper's Magazine* (November 1999), 12.

2. Karl Menninger M.D., *Whatever Became of Sin?* (New York: Hawthorn Books, Inc., 1973), 18-19.

4. Paul Tillich, "You Are Accepted," quoted in Karl Menninger, 47.

5. *Oxford Review* (July/August 1993).

6. Wendell Berry, *What Are People For?* (Berkeley, Calif.: North Point Press, 1990), 201.

7. "An Invitation to Jubilee," published by Jubilee Ministries, 1640 Columbia Road NW, Washington, D.C., 20009.

8. Douglas John Hall, *Why Christian? For Those on the Edge of Faith* (Minneapolis: Fortress Press, 1998), 47.

9. Roger Thurow, "South Africa Shows Just How Tricky Is Reconciliation's Path," *The Wall Street Journal*, July 17, 2000.